EXPERIENCE IT FOR YOURSELF!

Presented by **E. Lonnie Melashenko**
Written by **Ken Wade**

Pacific Press® Publishing Association
Nampa, Idaho
Oshawa, Ontario, Canada

Edited by B. Russell Holt
Cover design by Tim Larson
Cover photo Justinen Creative Group ©

Unless otherwise credited, all Scripture quotations
are from the New King James Version of the Bible.

Copyright © 2001 by
Pacific Press® Publishing Association
Printed in the United States of America
All Rights Reserved

ISBN 0-8163-1851-4

01 02 03 04 05 • 5 4 3 2 1

Contents

Introduction 5

Joy All the Time? 7

Face to Face With the Judge 13

Is It OK to Party Hearty? 19

Joy Hard Won 25

The Gift of Joy 30

The Gift of Laughter 36

A Laughing Jesus? 39

Ultimate Joy 47

Joy That Reaches Me 53

Lasting Joy 63

In October, 2000, the Voice of Prophecy broadcast team began production of a series of four programs we called "The Joy of Jesus." It proved to be a life-changing experience for all of us, as you'll discover as you read our personal testimonies, excerpts from interviews with people like Joni Eareckson Tada and Bruce Marchiano, and most importantly, the things we learned by looking at the life of Jesus.

Whether your life's been a little short on joy lately, or whether you're just a natural, bubbly, overflowing-with-happiness type, we hope you'll find new sources of true, deep joy as you read this little book.

    Ken Wade, writer-producer
    Lonnie Melashenko, director-speaker
    Connie Vandeman Jeffery, announcer
    David B. Smith, writer-producer

Joy All the Time?
Ken Wade

Is it possible to be joyful all the time?
Should we be?
We've all heard that text about "Rejoice in the Lord always, and again I say rejoice," and probably most of us have sung that song over and over again as a round at a youth meeting or praise service where a pastor with a big, Grand Canyon smile led the music and reminded us that as Christians we can always be happy, no matter what comes our way.

Someone else at that same meeting probably quoted Romans 8:28, reminding you that all things work together for good for those who love the Lord. So no matter how rotten your luck has been lately, or how much pain you endure every morning when you struggle out of bed, you ought to go around with a smile on your face and tell everyone you meet how happy it makes you to be a Christian.

And yet for all of us there are mornings when we get up without a smile. There are days that we go through, shell-shocked, wondering when the pain or sorrow will end.

And there are others of us who are kind of serious by nature. Our smiles are hard-won. Even when things are going fine, we tend to go around deep in thought, with a serious, or even somber, expression on our face. What would the apostle Paul think of us?

Is it possible to be have a deep-down joy that transcends all of these things—a joy that doesn't necessarily bubble over all the time in smiles, guffaws, and hallelujahs?

Connie Jeffery and I talked about that on one of the programs in the *Joy of Jesus* series. I confessed to her that I've been accused of going around looking kind of stern. In fact, when our family lived in Singapore for a few years, my wife pulled me aside one time and told me I needed to lighten up a bit. "All the secretaries in the office here are scared of you," she said. "They think you're really serious or something."

I had to think about that for a while—what made them see me that way? And then I realized that I do tend to hurry around from place to place when I'm working on a project, usually thinking about what needs to be done next. And even when I was a little boy, my mother had to tell me to quit frowning so much. It wasn't that I was angry; I just wrinkle my brow and look pretty serious when I'm thinking about something.

But Connie also pointed out that the dictionary definition of joy is "intense happiness," and I guess a person couldn't really go around acting *intensely* happy all the time. You'd just wear out after a while.

And that thought brought to mind a sermon I preached as a young pastor in Wisconsin. I, and most of my church members, had just returned from the annual camp meeting—a time when Christians from all over the state and points beyond get together and live in little cabins and tents for a week and listen to some of the world's best preachers.

I spent some time watching people that week, and later I reported my findings to my congregation in a sermon that must have had something to do with joy or happiness. I remember asking the question "Why is it that the only people I saw going around with smiles on their faces were the mentally retarded?" (We still used terms like that back in those days.)

Does one have to be short on mental capacity to be happy? Are the cares and concerns of the world so heavy on all of us who have our wits about us that we can seldom manage a real heartfelt smile?

Or is it perhaps true that Christians should be somber all the time? After all, if we're really walking with Jesus and really studying our Bibles, that will make us aware of our own sinfulness, the seriousness of the times we're living in, and impending judgment. Maybe we should be walking around looking depressed and calling the world to repentance. I've actually been told that by some Christians.

But I discovered something really interesting recently while preparing a program about the book of Nehemiah in the Old Testament.

Nehemiah lived in Persia. He was a Jew who had

found his way into the civil service of the Persian Empire. In fact he was cupbearer to King Artaxerxes I, who reigned from 465-423 B.C.

In 445 B.C. Nehemiah heard that the walls of Jerusalem had been broken down and its gates burned with fire, and he requested the king's permission to go and see what he could do about it. Artaxerxes appointed him governor of Jerusalem and sent him on his way. On his arrival, Nehemiah quickly rallied the Jews living in the area and put them to work. In fifty-two days they repaired the wall all the way around the city, just in time for the most solemn and important month on the Hebrew calendar—the seventh month.

In fact, they completed the wall just as autumn began on September 21, 444 B.C. Four days later, the thin silver crescent of the new moon hung in the western sky for a few minutes just after sundown, signifying the beginning of the month Tishri. It was a time for blowing trumpets and solemn assembly. All the able-bodied males of Israel were to report to Jerusalem for the ceremonies leading up to the tenth of the month, known as Yom Kippur, or the Day of Atonement.

As the crowd assembled near the temple, the scribe Ezra climbed the steps, stood on a low wooden platform, and solemnly opened the scrolls containing the law of God. As he opened the Scriptures, the whole congregation—men, women, and children—stood to their feet in reverence. They stood there all morning—until noon—listening to Ezra read. Levites and other educated people mingled with the crowd, explaining the things they were hearing. And what the people heard disturbed them deeply because the law pointed out their sins.

Nehemiah 8:9 tells us that "all the people wept, when they heard the words of the Law."

But here's the exciting thing that I discovered. Remember, this was all happening in the seventh month—just before the Day of Atonement (or day of judgment!) And here's what Nehemiah told the people when he saw them weeping about their sins: " 'This day is holy to the LORD your God; do not mourn nor weep. . . . Go your way, eat the fat, drink the sweet, and send portions to those for whom nothing is prepared; for this day is holy to our LORD. Do not sorrow, for the joy of the LORD is your strength' " (Nehemiah 8:9, 10).

Did you catch that? "The *joy* of the LORD is your strength."

I've sung that song too; haven't you? But did you know it came from Nehemiah's instructions to God's people about how to behave as they approached the day of judgment? I didn't know that before. But now that I do, I have a ready answer for those who tell me I ought to be somber and sad all the time because of conditions in the world and the impending judgment.

But there's another answer to those folks as well. And it's Jesus' answer. I must confess that when I first heard that the *Matthew* video series produced by The Visual Bible portrayed Jesus as a man of great joy, I was a bit suspicious. Wasn't that a bit shallow? Didn't Jesus go about telling people to repent because the kingdom of heaven was at hand? Should we really portray Him as a joyful Savior? I wondered.

Then I started reading the Gospels more carefully. And do you know what I discovered? Well, read on, and consider what happened when a man called Lev came face to face with the repentance-preaching Savior. . . .

Face to Face With the Judge
Ken Wade

His name was Lev. He sat behind a table, collecting money. All day long, that's what he did—just sat behind the table, waiting for people to bring him money. He wasn't a businessman who gave people merchandise in exchange for their money. He wasn't a clerk at a 7-11 store standing behind a counter, handing out cigarettes and soft drinks in exchange for people's money. He just sat behind his table and took the money and handed out receipts.

Fishermen who had toiled hard all night—on their feet, out on the lake, risking their lives doing backbreaking work—would come ashore with their catch. If they sold the rewards of their sweat and good fortune for a hundred dollars, they couldn't take it all home with them. First they had to go over to Lev's place and line up in front of his table, waiting their turn to give him six or seven of their hard-earned dollars.

The Roman tax on produce was only 5 percent, but every tax collector worth his salt knew how to tack

14 THE JOY OF JESUS

on an extra percentage point or two to enrich himself.

And what did people get in exchange for the money they gave to Lev? Not even a smile or a thank you. Lev could just sit there, six days a week, taking in the money, growing fat and lazy, profiting from other people's hard work.

That was enough to make his neighbors hate him and the local preachers condemn him. But there was something worse yet about Lev. He was a collaborator.

Maybe you've seen documentaries, as I have, of events that took place in 1944 and 1945 when cities in France were liberated from Nazi control by Allied troops. Most of the French people rejoiced. But there were some who were not happy—the opportunists who had cooperated fully with the Nazis. Now they were condemned as "collaborators," and justice came quickly from their neighbors—often in the form of a noose about the neck or a bullet in the forehead!

Yes, Lev was a collaborator, but the army of occupation was still in control, so he was safe from revenge—for the time being. But not safe from his neighbors' resentment.

Lev's tax table made him wealthy, but at the expense of the town's respect. Some would say at the cost of his very soul.

The tax table where he sat day after day, raking in the money, separated him from his community, from his religion, and—if he were to believe the teachings of the religious authorities—even from

FACE TO FACE WITH THE JUDGE 15

his God. It can't have been a very satisfying life.

Lev—we usually call him Levi-Matthew (or just Matthew)—lived 2,000 years ago, but people still face the same sort of dilemma he faced: the choice between making a lot of money or living a satisfying life. Valerie Young, publisher of the *Changing Course Newsletter,* shared the dilemma insightfully recently in an essay:

> My nephew Jason was pretty excited about starting college. "Do you have any idea what you'd like to do when you graduate?" I asked.
>
> "Something in the sciences," he said adding, "and where I can make a lot of money."
>
> "Is that all?" I asked.
>
> Jason paused for a moment before replying. "Well, I just hope I can find a job I don't hate too much."
>
> Time for a little auntie-to-nephew pep talk. "You have your whole life to look forward to," I said. "Don't you think you should shoot higher than just short of miserable?"
>
> Jason looked confused. "What should I be shooting for?"
>
> Clearly I was going to have to spell it out. "Satisfaction, fulfillment, meaning, you know—HAPPINESS!"
>
> By the look on my dear nephew's face I knew he wasn't buying it. This got me thinking about the great debate raging in the hearts and minds of many working adults today: Money vs. Happiness.

16 THE JOY OF JESUS

Valerie shares a modern perspective on Levi-Matthew's dilemma. She uses a powerful metaphor later in the essay when she calls a good salary and a retirement plan "golden handcuffs" that shackle people to unsatisfying jobs and stress-filled lives.

Day after day, Matthew sat behind that table—that golden table. In my mind's eye, I can see the legs of that table turning to gold—golden bars that imprisoned Matthew in an ever-darkening dungeon of disillusionment and despair. No one who came to that table left wishing him, "Have a nice day!" No. Everyone looked at him with hatred, wishing he'd curl up and die so they wouldn't have to part with their hard-earned money.

Matthew's tax booth became a vortex of despair and darkness, sucking the life and joy out of all who came there—and most of all out of Matthew himself.

But his booth was near enough to the shore that he could observe what was happening down by the Sea of Galilee. Suddenly one day, people began coming by with smiles on their faces. Why, some even smiled at *him!*

Then there was the lame beggar who hobbled down to the dock one morning and in the afternoon came running up the street laughing, smiling, singing, shouting the praises of God. He even stopped and did a little whirling dance of joy right in front of Matthew's table.

You couldn't help but notice that kind of thing. The whole atmosphere of Capernaum was changing. Fewer people shook their fists and glared at Matthew when they saw him on the street. There seemed

FACE TO FACE WITH THE JUDGE 17

to be a sunlit spot, somewhere down by the lake, where people's lives were being changed—recharged—and filled with joy!

Soon Matthew discovered that at the center of that sunlit spot stood a Man. A Man whose life radiated joy, healing, forgiveness, and satisfaction even more powerfully than Matthew's life reeked of illness, unforgiven debts, and frustration.

There came a day when Matthew slipped out from behind his table—just for a few moments—and went to listen.

The Teacher spoke of love, kindness, and forgiveness—words that floated on the fresh, spring air like butterflies of happiness. They almost brightened even Matthew's face.

But then he realized that such things were not for him. Forgiveness was for the righteous—those who devoted their lives to memorizing and reciting the Law—not for the likes of him. Not for sinful, despised, outcast tax collectors.

The smile that had toyed with the corners of his mouth flitted away, and Matthew trudged back to his little booth, behind the golden bars of his tax table, and sat down once again in the dark dungeon of despair.

Head hanging, he hardly noticed the excitement that began to brew around his booth, but when he did look up, he discovered that the Teacher had followed him. The Teacher was standing at his tax table! And suddenly the atmosphere of that dark vortex of despair seemed changed, recharged, filled with light and happiness.

He looked up into the Teacher's face, and the Teacher returned his gaze. And then He spoke two words: "Follow Me."

"Follow Me?" How could a sinner like me follow a Teacher of righteousness? Why does He want me to come with Him? I am so far from God.... The questions tumbled through Matthew's mind, but all seemed to be answered in a microsecond in the smile and wide-open arms of the Man who had invited him.

None of the questions, none of the doubts, none of the despair had any relevance anymore. The Teacher had invited him. The Teacher had accepted him. The Teacher—Jesus—wanted him!

"And Levi [Matthew] rose and followed him" (Mark 2:14, NEB).

There was joy in Matthew's heart, and there was joy in Jesus' heart. Joy that would soon overflow in a celebration—a party—that would shake the foundations of the city.

We'll consider Matthew's celebration in our next chapter. But before we do, take a minute to think about yourself in relation to the Matthew's story. Where are you in relation to Jesus—in relation to God? Is there something that is imprisoning you, keeping you from Him? Does your life seem somehow like a dark dungeon? If so, Jesus wants to bring His light and His joy in. He wants to break the bars that imprison you.

He comes to you today, like He did to Matthew so many years ago, and says, "Follow Me."

Is It OK to Party Hearty?
Ken Wade

What was the pastor's wife doing in a strip bar? The answer in a moment, but first another question: What if it had been the *pastor* instead of his wife that was seen going into that place of ill repute? Would you assume he was having a moral fall, or would you think he was going in to share his faith?

Let's phrase the question a little differently. If you're a Christian, would you consider a seedy strip lounge a good place to do your witnessing? Could you picture Jesus going into a place like that to share the good news of the kingdom?

Well, before you get the wrong idea from the questions I'm asking, let me hasten to add that it *was* the pastor's *wife,* not the pastor himself, who was seen going into a strip bar in Orlando, Florida a few months ago. And I'm glad to report that the dear lady had a good reason for going in. There are appropriate places for a Christian to share her faith, but as a male pastor, I'm not sure it would be wise for me to try to witness in a strip bar. We hear too many reports of pastors and other religious leaders who have had their ministry ruined by such things. We shouldn't set ourselves up for that kind of temptation and fall.

But I have to say that I admire those women—delegates to a recent Southern Baptist convention in Orlando—who volunteered to take part in a special evangelistic outreach to the female employees of the city's strip joints. These dedicated Christian women went into the bars, carrying gold coins in their purses to share with the female employees. They went in with a mission—to speak to a woman, share their testimony, and give her a dollar coin. On one side, these new gold-colored coins have a picture of Sacagawea, the woman who guided Lewis and Clark, and an eagle on the other side. The Christian women gave out the coins, reminding their listeners: "To God, you are more precious than gold. This coin is a gift to you so you'll remember the strength you have as a woman and your ability to soar like an eagle."

That story impressed me because it reminds me of Jesus and how He is willing to meet people where they are and point them to something better.

Matthew was a tax collector. One of the most despised people in the village of Capernaum. He was a collaborator who had sold his soul to the Roman army of occupation. No one liked him. No one spoke kindly to him. As far as the religious authorities were concerned, he had headed down the road to hell when he chose his profession, and that's where he was going to end up.

IS IT OK TO PARTY HEARTY? 21

Then one day the new preacher, Jesus, came by his tax booth. He didn't wait for Matthew to come to church or an evangelistic series. Maybe Jesus had seen the tax collector on the fringes of the crowds that flocked to hear Him preach—standing on the edges, listening, wishing that somehow he could be part of the wonderful kingdom Jesus talked about.

But Matthew hadn't come forward at an altar call. He had watched the lame and maimed go to Jesus and leave restored and whole, and he may have wished that a mere touch could heal a wounded soul as well. But he knew it couldn't be so easy. Not for someone like him. So he had never gone forward to talk with Jesus.

But Jesus didn't wait for him to. Jesus didn't wait for Matthew to reach out and ask for healing. He went right to Matthew's tax booth—that dungeon of despair where Matthew sat, imprisoned by his choices, enslaved by his wealth.

And Jesus looked right over top of Matthew's tax table and said those two words: "Follow Me."

It was as though an eagle had swooped down and lifted Matthew, soaring into the sky, raising him high above the despair and darkness that had entombed his life.

All the resistance, all the condemnation, all the doubts peeled away like a cocoon falling from a butterfly, and Matthew spread his wings and soared too.

The news that he—the chief of sinners in his city—could be forgiven and could start a new life following God was almost too good to be true. But Jesus' smiling eyes told him it was true.

Matthew jumped to his feet, leaving the old behind, leaving the *gold* behind, and pursuing the true wealth of the kingdom of God.

And the good news of God's love for him, a sinner, was too good to keep to himself. That's why he threw the party that shook the social and religious foundations of Capernaum.

It was the happiest day of his life. He just *had* to share it with someone! Jesus had accepted him into the kingdom of God! If Jesus could accept *him*—well, what about all the other tax collectors and sinners in town? Wouldn't they want to know that they could be forgiven and be a part of the kingdom too?

And so the invitations went out. Servants hurrying from mansion to mansion and out into the alleys and byways, proclaimed the good news—to the wealthy and the winos, to the prostitutes and even to the pimps: Matthew's throwing a party at his house, and you're invited! Free food! Free drink! Music and singing! Come one, come all!

And so they came in droves. The wealthy and powerful, and also the lowlifes of the town—all the profligates and prodigals who would never darken the door of a church or synagogue—flocked to the feast. Because Matthew wanted to introduce them to his new best friend, Jesus. Jesus, who would offer them forgiveness and a place in the kingdom of God.

They couldn't believe it when they saw Jesus at the party. Wasn't He that pious preacher who went around telling people to repent? What was He doing here?

Jesus was at Matthew's party just like He had been

IS IT OK TO PARTY HEARTY? 23

at Matthew's tax booth. He was there with the smiling, joyful eyes, looking into the face of sinner after sinner and saying "God loves you and wants you as part of His kingdom!"

That was just too much for the scribes and Pharisees. They knew that religion is stern stuff. It's tough business. It requires sacrifice, fasting, and strict, disciplined self-denial. There's no room for party going, reveling, or happiness. They questioned some of Jesus' disciples: " 'Why does [Jesus] eat with tax collectors and "sinners"?' " (Mark 2:16, NIV).

How did Jesus respond? Did He suddenly realize just whom He had been hanging out with and what a bad impression it might make? Did He hurry out of the party and apologize for the bad example He was setting?

No. He had a simple answer for the Pharisees: " 'It is not the healthy who need a doctor, but the sick. I have not come to call the righteous, but sinners' " (Mark 2:17, NIV).

Jesus didn't apologize for His joy. He didn't apologize for going to a party to look men and women in the eye and tell them that their heavenly Father loved them and wanted something better for them—wanted to invite them to His heavenly banquet.

Jesus wanted His joy—the joy of knowing a God of love—to spread. And so He shared that love with those who needed it most: those who had wandered farthest from it.

I just wonder: Is it possible that you feel something like Matthew and his friends felt? Is it possible that for some reason you feel that you're too low in the social or spiritual order to be important to Jesus—too far from God to be saved in His kingdom?

If you're ever tempted to feel that way, take a moment to consider Jesus' own words: " 'I have not come to call the righteous, but sinners.' " Picture Him there at that feast thrown in His honor by Matthew. Picture Him reaching out to all the sinners, the downtrodden of society.

Do you see the love in His eyes? Do you see the joy He wants to share with you? Remember, He created you to be joyful.

You can receive Him. You can receive the joy of Jesus.

"But, you don't know what my life is like," I hear someone saying, "You don't know what I've been through. It's fine and dandy for you to say that I ought to be joyful. But wait till you've walked a few miles in my moccasins and then see what you say."

Well, I don't have an answer for you—because I haven't been in your shoes. But I know someone who does have an answer. We went to her office and spoke with her about how she finds joy every day. And she hasn't had the privilege of walking—even in her own shoes—for more than thirty years. Read on, as Connie Jeffery tells you about meeting this remarkable woman.

Joy Hard Won
Connie Jeffery

Most of us remember the story of Joni, the young teenager who found herself paralyzed from the shoulders down following a diving accident. Before I met her, I thought I knew all about her. But I was wrong. There is much more to this woman who has maintained a positive Christian ministry from a wheelchair for the past thirty years than the story of a teenager and a tragic accident.

That gray December afternoon when Ken and I drove over to the offices of her "Joni and Friends" ministry in Agoura Hills, California, I was a little apprehensive. After all, we were there to interview her about "joy." To be perfectly honest, I didn't feel all that joyful myself that day. Maybe if I just asked her the right questions, she would do all the talking, and we would have our interview. Maybe I could kind of fake being joyful, and she would carry the interview and get the concept across to our listeners.

That would certainly work, I thought. What I didn't count on was that her joy was absolutely, positively contagious! I left feeling not only incredibly blessed to have met her, but full of a sense of peace and comfort—and yes, even, joy—that I hadn't felt for some time.

The reason I wasn't full of joy on that December day was that it had been less than a month since we had laid my dear father, Pastor George Vandeman, to rest. After the whirlwind of activity surrounding the funeral service and the myriad of details to attend to following his death, I felt myself sinking into a sadness, and maybe a touch of depression, that I just couldn't shake. I put on a brave, cheerful face at work and in my daily life, but there was a void in my heart and a feeling of joylessness. I missed him so very much.

Keeping up my work schedule and recording the weekend VOP broadcasts with Lonnie helped to lift my spirits during that time, but I was beginning to feel a little sorry for myself. God had given me the strength to get through the initial few days and weeks following Dad's death, but would He be there in some of the dark days ahead? Would He be able to put a smile on my face once again? Intellectually, I knew He would, but emotionally, I started to doubt that I'd ever feel real joy again. Then I met Joni.

Ken found an article that Joni had written for *Decision* magazine entitled "Joy Hard Won." That became the basis for our interview. She knew that we were in the middle of a series on "The Joy of Jesus" and was more than willing to set aside an hour of her day to talk with us. We set up the microphones and recorder in her conference room, and a few minutes later Joni breezed into the room propelling herself in a high-tech electronic wheelchair. She looked stunningly beautiful in her black wool turtleneck sweater, with every hair in place and her makeup perfectly applied. What struck me immediately was her gorgeous smile and her kind, penetrating eyes. They were filled with joy!

We exchanged introductions, and Joni was the first to suggest that we ask God to bless our efforts. Ken had already turned on the tape recorder, and by the end of her simple, but powerful prayer, I was beginning to catch some of her joy. Let me share just a part of that prayer with you:

> Days like this are always wonderful, Lord Jesus, when the clouds hang heavy on the coastal mountains, and it's a gray day. It reminds us that change is helpful and that variety is always a gift from You. And these clouds remind us that there are showers of blessing that come from Your heaven. We thank you for these dear friends who are going to be sharing some incredible insights about Your joy! And, Lord Jesus, it occurs to us that we're a bunch of sour-faced people who get grumpy and irritated, and yet your joy is so powerful. You are the high Hoover Dam of Joy! It's spilling and splashing over heaven's walls, and we just seem so satisfied to drink from a mud puddle. So please help us to appreciate Your joy by the insights shared today. And now give us Your words, we ask in Your name. Amen.

In "Joy Hard Won," Joni tells of an experience at a Christian women's conference where she was the speaker. She was in the restroom when a woman, putting on lipstick, turned to her and said, "Oh Joni, you always look so together, so happy in your wheelchair. I wish I had your joy!" Several women around her nodded and asked, "How do you do it?"

I asked her that same question, and the answer that followed filled the rest of our five-minute interview. Her answer to the question, "How do you do it?" was simply this: "I don't do it." That response raised some eyebrows in the restroom that day. Then she went on to describe her average day.

"This is an average day," she said. "After my husband Ken leaves for work at 6:00 a.m., I'm alone until I hear the front door open at 7:00 a.m. That's when a friend arrives to get me up.

"While I listen to her come in, shut the door, and then run water for coffee, I begin to pray, 'Lord Jesus, my friend will soon give me a bath, get me dressed, sit me in my chair, brush my hair and teeth, and send me out the door. I don't have the strength to face this routine one more time. I have no resources. I don't have a smile to take into the day, but You do. May I have yours? God, I need You desperately.'"

"And does He give you that smile?" I ask, already knowing her answer, but completely taken with her presence and her joy.

Joni continues, "I turn my head toward my friend and give her a smile sent straight from heaven. It's not mine. It's God's. Whatever joy you see today was hard won this morning."

Joni went on to describe how the weaker we are, the more we need to learn to lean on God. And the more we lean on God, the stronger we will discover Him to be.

I totally forgot about myself and my loss during that precious hour with Joni. And in forgetting about *me* and learning in a fresh, new way that I needed to keep my eyes focused on Jesus, I began to catch some of Joni's joy.

Maybe the "harder won" the joy, the more it is appreciated. Here in front of me was a woman who epitomized the very concept of joy.

At the end of our interview, Ken took some photos of Joni and me in her art studio. Before we left, we gave her some Voice of Prophecy material, and I had brought along a copy of my dad's book, *My Dream*.

"I don't know if you've heard of my father or not," I said as I offered her his book, "but he was a television evangelist for many years, and he just passed away. I'd like you to have this."

"George Vandeman!" she exclaimed as she looked at his picture on the front cover. "I used to watch *It Is Written* when I was lying in a hospital bed in Baltimore, Maryland, when I would flip through the dials looking for religious programs."

I left Joni's office feeling incredibly blessed and not even the teeniest bit sorry for myself anymore. We all experience sadness and the loss of precious loved ones. She just reminded me that God, the source of all joy, would always be there for me to put that smile back on my face!

The Gift of Joy
Ken Wade

The handicapped man (since we don't know his name, we'll make one up; let's call him Zach) moved unnoticed through the crowd that was gathering at the synagogue. He slipped into his customary seat, waiting for the beginning of prayers. There was nothing remarkable about the event, and no one paid him any mind, for he was not among the wealthy or learned. Just a humble man—half a man in some people's eyes—barely able to eke out a subsistence with that crippled hand.

It was an ordinary Sabbath day, and he didn't expect anything out of the ordinary to happen. He didn't expect to leave there restored and filled with joy. But he would. Because this was no ordinary day. Extraordinary things were about to happen.

The extraordinary had already begun—outside the synagogue in a wheat field. The new, young rabbi had been on His way to that same synagogue, walking through the field, when some of His followers had reached out and grabbed a few heads of ripened wheat, rubbed them together in their hands, and let the chaff drop to the ground before popping the kernels into their mouths.

Such an act would have passed unnoticed on any other day, but this was not to be an ordinary day. It was to be a day of liberation, a day of joy, a day of healing—an *extra*ordinary day. But before that, it would be a day of confrontation.

The scribes and Pharisees had been following Jesus and His disciples like a pack of paparazzi pursuing a politician, waiting for Him to make some little mistake to be written up in the morning's headlines.

These were the same guys who'd criticized Jesus for attending Matthew's celebration two days earlier—who'd tried to make it look like He was less holy than they were since they were fasting while He was feasting. But, as usual, Jesus had had a ready response for them, and they had left that encounter bested, embarrassed, and all the more angry. They were all the more determined to catch Him in some infraction of the law—something they could use to accuse Him of being a lawbreaker and an unworthy teacher.

They got their chance when they spotted Jesus' disciples picking and eating grain out in the field on the way to the synagogue. According to the Pharisees, the disciples had broken the Sabbath four ways that morning: reaping the grain, threshing it, winnowing it, and sorting it.

They were quick with their accusations: "And the Pharisees said to [Jesus], 'Look, why do they [His disciples] do what is not lawful on the Sabbath?' " (Mark 2:24).

They wanted to make Jesus out to be a lawbreaker, or a libertine—a radical free-thinker. That way they could discredit Him and turn the people away from Him.

But as usual, Jesus was ready for them. In fact, He was one step ahead of them. He and His disciples stopped at the edge of the field and delayed their trip to the synagogue long enough for Jesus to tell the Pharisees a little story.

Didn't they remember their Bible history? He asked. Hadn't they read about the time that David and his followers were hungry. What had they done? They'd gone to the tabernacle and eaten some of the holy bread that was supposed to be reserved only for the priests. And neither the priests nor God had condemned them for it.

There was a lesson to be learned from that story: Rules and regulations have their place. But God is more interested in meeting people's needs than He is in rules and regulations.

Then, having told the story, Jesus and His disciples continued on their journey to the synagogue where Zach was. To where Zach was about to have a date with destiny. An encounter that would change his life and fill him with joy.

When he came into the synagogue, no one else had paid any attention to Zach, the man with the crippled hand. But Jesus paid attention. And when He did, so did everyone else.

Jesus loved to heal people. He loved to see their lives changed, their bodies restored, their spirits raised to new levels of joy. And He wanted to do that for Zach.

THE GIFT OF JOY 33

But as He looked around the synagogue, He knew that was not what the Pharisees wanted. They didn't care a thing about Zach or his crippled hand. All they cared about was enforcing rules and regulations—especially if they could use those rules to discredit Jesus and make Him look like a lawbreaker.

All eyes turned to Jesus. What would He do?

Now, this book is about "The Joy of Jesus," but I want you to notice something here in the middle of this story in Mark 3: "Then Jesus asked them, 'Which is lawful on the Sabbath: to do good or to do evil, to save life or to kill?' But they remained silent. He looked around at them *in anger* and, deeply distressed at their stubborn hearts . . ." (Mark 3:4, 5, NIV, emphasis supplied).

Yes, Jesus got angry. In fact the word translated "anger" here is actually the word for "wrath." Jesus was really upset! Disgusted that people could have such hard hearts.

Not much made Jesus angry. But self-righteous, uncaring, judgmental, holier-than-thou hypocrites really got to Him. Because He really cared about people. And when you really care, you get upset when people are treated as something less than human.

Jesus looked at the Pharisees in anger.

But He looked at Zach with a smile. With loving eyes. With a soft voice. And He said four simple words: "Stretch out your hand." And the man "stretched it out, and his hand was completely restored" (verse 5, NIV).

Now, the Bible story doesn't tell us how Zach responded. It doesn't tell us about the joy that must have filled his heart. It doesn't tell us how his family reacted when they saw him healed. But there must have been a lot of joy in Capernaum that day.

The Bible doesn't tell us how Jesus responded either—but can't you see Him looking into the eyes of that man who has just had his hand fully restored, and sharing a smile, an exclamation of excitement, a sentence or two of praise to God, an expression of joy?

Jesus loved to spread joy wherever He went.

What the Bible *does* tell us is how the Pharisees responded. Here it is in Mark 3:6: "Then the Pharisees went out and began to plot with the Herodians how they might kill Jesus" (NIV).

They wanted to kill Him!

Why?

Just because He had healed a man on the Sabbath?

No. That healing there in the synagogue was just the last straw. It was just one more instance of Jesus refusing to fit within the narrow set of rules that the religious authorities enforced.

You see, the scribes and Pharisees saw religion one way, and Jesus saw it quite another.

Jesus had made the point very clearly out in the wheat field.

When the Pharisees accused the disciples of breaking the Sabbath commandment by popping a few grains of wheat into their mouths, Jesus responded by telling them that " 'The Sabbath was made for man, not man for the Sabbath' " (Mark 2:27, NIV).

Do you catch the significance of that simple statement?

You see, the Pharisees treated the Sabbath commandment, and all of God's commandments, like a list of *don't*s—a compendium of things one shouldn't do.

They made the Sabbath out to be a day God had created for Himself. A day He kept for Himself. A day that He had taken away from mankind. It was a debit from man's account. One day in seven in which people couldn't do what they wanted.

But Jesus reversed that. Notice, He said: "The Sabbath was made *for* man." It was not a debit from our account, but a credit—a gift from God!

The Sabbath was God's gift to Adam and Eve. A whole day that God was "taking off" to spend with His kids! A day of joy for all creation, because it was time to spend with the beloved Creator.

For Jesus, the Sabbath was not a solemn day of "don'ts." It was a joyful day of "dos." Do good. Help others. Spend time with your heavenly Father, learning to be more like Him.

The Pharisees saw the law as a "Cease and Desist" order. Jesus saw it as a "Do and Delight" privilege.

"Take the Sabbath day," He said. "God has given it to you as a gift. Use it as a time for learning to delight in the things of God and in doing the works of God. Use it to restore, to heal, to bring joy."

And friend, it's not only the Sabbath that Jesus wants us to see that way. He wants us to learn to see all of God's laws that way. They are His gift to you—to bring joy into your life.

And there's another gift He's given as well—a gift that He has given only to human beings. It's a gift that's all wrapped up in joy. Do you know what it is? David Smith will tell you in the next chapter.

The Gift of Laughter
David B. Smith

I guess there's nothing funny about being a chimpanzee. Oh, they can bounce around and play and drive little fire engines and out-act Clint Eastwood or Ronald Reagan in a Hollywood movie. But the latest word from the men in the white coats is that when Bonzo gives you a belly laugh, it's actually just rhythmic panting. One sound per inhale and exhale. That's in contrast to us humans, who have—they say—evolved to the point that we can "chop up a single exhalation into multiple bursts of 'ha ha ha.' " This is according to neuroscientist Robert Provine, whose new book, *Laughter: A Scientific Investigation,* suggests that there are valid biological reasons why *homo sapiens* is the only species that really sits down to a rerun of *Everybody Loves Raymond* and actually laughs.

Believers in evolution also have a theory that you can't genuinely laugh unless you can walk upright on two legs. Clomping around on all fours makes it anatomically hard for our furry friends to "use their breath and vocal cords to make complex sounds" like ha ha ha. Their breathing patterns, and their four-legged gait while walking or running, mean that it takes all the air in a chimp's lungs just to keep his balance when his forelimbs hit the ground. There's no oxygen left for humor and jokes. All of this gives new meaning, of course, to the expression "stand-up comic."

Well, you know, you can buy into this theory about the "evolution of bipedalism." Or you can decide, instead, that the only reason us humans enjoy a good joke—and not the animals—is because a loving God, with a smile on His face, made us the one fortunate species, created in His image, that could laugh. Laughter "doeth good like a medicine," we read in Proverbs. And G. K. Chesterton once observed, "Joy is the gigantic secret of the Christian."

And really, it's been true since Eden that nobody likes to laugh alone. "God is enjoying Himself," writes Meister Eckhart, "and He expects us to join Him." Which is why He got down in the dirt, made a two-legged man, stepped back, scratched His head, and then said: "Ah . . . I can do better than that." And made the second half of the comedy team of Adam and Eve.

Now, I don't know how you react to the idea that Adam and Eve were a comedy team. But don't you suppose that there were many times in their centuries-long marriage that they exercised the privilege God had given to them alone of all His creation—the gift of laughter?

Yes, I think Adam and Eve had a lot of laughter in their lives.

But what about Jesus.

Can you picture Jesus laughing? Taking advantage of this gift He Himself gave to the human race?

Read on.

A Laughing Jesus?
Ken Wade

I remember hearing two people arguing once about whether Jesus ever laughed. And neither of them was smiling.

It set me to thinking, though. I never came up with a definite answer until one morning as I sat at my computer with tears streaming down my face as I retold a familiar Bible story in a new way.

No, I don't usually talk to my computer. I usually tell it stories with my fingers flying over its keyboard. More than three years ago I set myself the challenge of telling a story about Jesus in a new way at least once a week and sending it out via email to anyone who wanted to read it. The mailing list has grown through the years, and now hundreds of people all around the world receive my fresh take on the gospel every week. (If you'd like to receive this weekly devotional message via email, see the instructions at the end of this chapter.)[1]

For several weeks I had been studying the events following the resurrection of Jesus, and this particular morning as I retold one particular story, I found myself crying—but they were tears of joy! Tears that welled up in my eyes and ran down my cheeks as I bent over, almost doubled up with laughter.

What could be so funny in a gospel story, you ask. Well, see if you can find it in the story below. I called the series of messages "The Third Call." Here are two of them (numbers eight and nine), focusing on the story told in John 21 of Jesus meeting the disciples at the Sea of Galilee after His resurrection.

* * * *

The Third Call—8

"Therefore that disciple whom Jesus loved said to Peter, 'It is the Lord!' Now when Simon Peter heard that it was the Lord, he put on his outer garment (for he had removed it), and plunged into the sea. But the other disciples came in the little boat (for they were not far from land, but about two hundred cubits), dragging the net with fish" (John 21:7, 8).

Why did Peter put his clothes *on* to go swimming?

According to *The Bible Almanac*, "Hebrew men wore an 'outer garment' consisting of a square or oblong strip of cloth, 2-3 meters (80 to 120 in.) wide. This garment (*me 'yil*) was called the *coat, robe, or mantle*. It was wrapped around the body as a protective covering, with two corners of the material being in front."[2]

Doesn't sound much like a swimming suit to me, does it to you?

I always assumed that it was out of respect for the Lord that Peter put on this cloak before swimming to shore—after all, you wouldn't want to go to see Jesus in your underwear, would you? But in fact, the inner garment Peter was wearing in the boat was quite common apparel for outdoor work. People working in the fields would not even have their cloak, or outer garment, with them (see Matthew 24:18).

The King James Version of the Bible says that Peter was "naked" in the boat. The New American Standard Bible has perhaps the most accurate translation: "(for he was stripped *for work)*." In other words, he was dressed like any workman or fisherman you might see daily in Palestine. He was dressed the way that He was when he received the second call from Jesus (see Luke 5:1-11). There was nothing shameful about his attire.

Earlier, as a prelude to that second call, Jesus had gotten into Peter's boat, after the disciples had spent another long, unsuccessful night fishing, and had told him to let down his nets in broad daylight—not a good time for that kind of fishing—and the nets were filled.

Now, after His resurrection, Jesus has worked a reprise of that miracle. Calling to the seven disciples in the boat, after their long, fruitless fishing expedition, He tells them, " 'Cast the net on the right side of the boat, and you will find some [food]' " (John 21:6).

The net fills with fish, and the disciples suddenly realize that it is Jesus' voice they hear coming to them across the water. Peter's immediate, impulsive response is to go to the Lord.

Now, bring another encounter between Jesus and Peter into this picture. Remember the story in Matthew 14 about Jesus calling across the water to a discouraged, disappointed group of disciples in a boat? Peter responded that time by saying " 'Lord, if it is You, command me to come to You on the water.' " (Matthew 14:28). And at Jesus' word Peter, walked on the water to go to his Master.

Picture it now. This time Peter is sure it's the Lord. He doesn't have to ask questions. He's a man of faith. He knows for sure what faith can do. And so what does he do? Does he dive into the water and swim to shore?

I don't think so. The picture I see is of a man dressing to go for a walk, not for a swim.

Can you see it? Go to the Bible and read the passage for yourself. Notice that it doesn't say anything about Peter swimming to shore. Notice that when the boat got to shore Peter "went up [not down] and dragged the net to land" (verse 11). In other words, he didn't swim ahead of the boat to shore.

I can see Peter, full of faith, throwing on his cloak, climbing onto the gunwales, and taking a bold step out onto the water. Plunging feet first straight to the bottom, fighting his way up, up, toward the light at the surface, grabbing onto the net full of fish behind the boat to pull himself gasping to the surface, coming up sputtering—a look of shock and utter consternation on his face.

Have you ever set out to go to the Lord, walking

by faith, ready to walk on water if need be, only to plunge to the depths? Take heart. Maybe it's part of the training school through which Jesus is leading you in preparation for your "third call."

* * * *

The Third Call—9

"But the other disciples came in the little boat (for they were not far from land, but about two hundred cubits), dragging the net with fish. . . . Simon Peter went up and dragged the net to land, full of large fish, one hundred and fifty-three; and although there were so many, the net was not broken" (John 21:8, 11).

In the last message we looked at Peter's plunge into the sea. I'm guessing that he never intended to have to swim to shore. He probably planned to walk on the water, as he had done before. But he ended up getting all wet.

And notice in verse 11 that John tells us "Peter went up and dragged the net to land." If Peter was already on the shore when the boat arrived, the account would no doubt picture him "going down" to the water to bring the net up. There's no mention of Peter making it to shore ahead of the boat, so the picture I get is of Peter coming up sputtering from his unexpected dunking, grabbing onto the net behind the boat, and being towed to shore. When the boat arrives, he comes up out of the water, pulling the net with him.

Now, let me ask you a question.

Can you picture Jesus laughing? What about

the disciples? Do you think they were all a bunch of serious old long-faces who never gave way to gales of laughter when someone told a funny story?

Well, you can follow me on this or not, but I like to picture this story with lots of laughter involved. I can see quick, impetuous Peter, throwing on his cloak, hastily girding it around himself, in his excitement getting one foot up on the gunwales before he even has his girdle tied right, then stepping up and out, and SPLASH!

The other disciples have hardly had time to figure out what's going on; they look over the edge of the boat, and all they can see is bubbles.

They look at each other, puzzled expressions on their faces. "What happened? Where's Peter gone now?"

And then finally, behind the boat, here he comes, spluttering to the surface, looking no less puzzled than the others, and a lot more chagrined.

I laughed so hard I had tears on my chin when I pictured the scene.

Can you see the other disciples roaring in laughter? Can you see Jesus on the shore, joining in, pointing His finger, doubling over, enjoying the joke on Peter? Can you see Peter, at first looking angry and embarrassed, maybe wounded, but finally giving way to a smirk, then a chuckle, and finally a wholehearted laugh?

I don't know. Maybe you have trouble with that picture. Maybe you can't see Jesus laughing at Peter's predicament. But I've learned enough about the Savior recently to realize that He enjoyed a good joke, or at least pulling surprises on people. I love the image of the laughing Jesus. It makes Him so much more human and lovable to me.

Jesus was preparing Peter for the third call, and there was an important lesson for the disciple to learn from this experience. Something we can learn too.

It's easy to assume that as long as we keep our eyes on Jesus, as long as we're walking toward Him, things should go our way. It's easy to think that because the Lord has blessed us once with a special gift (such as walking on water), He'll always give it to us when we think we need it.

But all of these things are gifts from the Lord. Not to be presumed upon. Sometimes it takes a cold dunking in reality to wake us up. Does God laugh at us as we come spluttering to the surface? I don't think He laughs at us, but He may laugh *with* us when we look back and remember.

* * * *

So, that's the conclusion I came to. Yes, I think Jesus could laugh—and that He enjoyed doing so. After all, He's the One who made us with a laugh reflex in the first place. So why would He refuse to use it? He enjoyed joining in with people in all their times of joy, as well as their times of sorrow. And He did whatever He could to keep the times joyful—as He did that Wednesday night in Cana, the night I want to tell you about in the next chapter.

1. If you would like to receive the weekly "Fresh Look at Jesus" devotional written by Ken Wade, send an email to freshlook@att.net with "subscribe" as the subject.

2. *The Bible Almanac,* James I. Packer, Merril C. Tenney, and William White, eds. (Nashville: Thomas Nelson Publishers, 1980), 480.

Ultimate Joy
Ken Wade

Wednesday night was party night in Cana. At least it was this particular Wednesday night, because a blushing young bride—probably a girl of about fifteen or so—was getting married. Her bridegroom, a young man a few years older than herself, had been betrothed to her sometime within the past few months through arrangements worked out between the two young people's fathers.

Jesus and Nathanael and Andrew and John and Peter and Philip had just arrived in town after a very long journey, and they were guests at the wedding. In fact it seems possible that the bride and groom may have been close friends of Jesus—maybe even relatives.

The story is told in the Gospel of John, chapter 2, but I don't think it starts there. There's a little bit of the story back in chapter 1 as well, I think. I'm referring to chapter 1, verse 43: "The following day Jesus wanted to go to Galilee, and He found Philip and said to him, 'Follow Me.'"

Jesus seemed to have had a schedule for getting to Galilee. John 2:1 tells us that "On the third day there was a wedding in Cana of Galilee." It seems likely that Jesus left the area where He had gathered His first disciples—down by the Jordan where John the Baptist was baptizing—just in time to make the three-day journey to Cana specifically to attend the wedding.

Now, notice something else about the prologue to the story of the wedding: "Philip found Nathanael and said to him, 'We have found Him of whom Moses in the law, and also the prophets, wrote—Jesus of Nazareth, the son of Joseph' " (1:45).

It's not mentioned here, but it just so happens that Nathanael's hometown was none other than Cana of Galilee! Maybe that's why Philip thought of him when Jesus decided to head for Galilee.

Anyhow, it seems clear that Jesus found His way to the wedding celebration on purpose. He didn't just happen into town at an opportune moment.

Would you walk for three days to get to a wedding? I'm not sure I would. But Jesus did. Because He wanted to be there to share in that joyful time with His friends! And, by the way, the distance He had to travel was far more than a three-day's journey. He and His disciples must have had to do double-time to get there before the celebration was over.

Do you suppose they were extra thirsty when they finally arrived? Do you suppose their thirst could have had anything to do with the crisis that developed— that threatened to spoil the festivities? Jesus' mother was invited to the wedding, and no doubt Jesus was too. But what about those five thirsty fellows He brought with Him. No host could turn them away, but what about the wine supply? Would it hold out with so many extra guests?

Now, just a word about the type of wine we're discussing here. There's been a lot of discussion through the years of whether Jesus drank fermented wine or not, and as I understand it, the words used in the original Greek can refer either to unfermented or fermented grape juice. People in those days did have ways of preserving unfermented juice, so it could have been either. But personally, I find it hard to picture Jesus, the Son of God, drinking wine that would intoxicate Him. How about you? I'm convinced that if Jesus was partaking of the wine, it wasn't the bubbly kind!

But whatever the rest of the crowd was drinking, it ran out far too early in the evening.

Picture the scene that unfolded when the master of ceremonies realized that the punch bowl was going dry. A wedding was a big event in a town like Cana—something people looked forward to and planned for months. It was an important time for the bridegroom's family to shine—to make a name for themselves in the community—by having the biggest, most successful celebration anyone could remember.

But if things went wrong—if the refreshments ran out, before the evening was over—well, just think of the gossip that would float around the town the next day and for weeks, maybe months, to come. It would be a humiliating situation—and one that could haunt the newlyweds for the rest of their lives. An unmitigated social disaster!

Jesus' mother soon became aware of the crisis-in-the-making, and somehow she thought that Jesus would know what to do about it. He was, after all, her oldest son, and apparently she was a widow by now, because Joseph isn't mentioned in this story.

Now, you've no doubt heard this story before, and you know what Jesus did. But just for a minute, try to read the story with new eyes. Try to imagine what was running through Mary's mind, and through Jesus' mind, as the following exchange took place:

"And when they ran out of wine, the mother of Jesus said to Him, 'They have no wine.' Jesus said to her, 'Woman, what does your concern have to do with Me? My hour has not yet come.' His mother said to the servants, 'Whatever He says to you, do it'" (John 2:3-5).

Stop for a moment now. Pretend you don't know the end of the story. Ask yourself: What did Mary expect Jesus to do about that situation? Did she expect a miraculous solution to the problem? Or was she, maybe, just suggesting gently to Jesus "You know, you're the one that brought the five extra guests. Maybe you ought to send someone out to get some more punch!" Were her words to the servants "Whatever He says to you, do it" simply her way of authorizing them to follow Jesus' instructions to go buy more wine and put it on the family's tab?

I don't know what Mary expected. I don't know what the servants expected or what the host expected. But I do know that they got something much better

ULTIMATE JOY 51

than they could ever have hoped for. Because Jesus turned water to wine—new, fresh, invigorating, sweet wine—the best anyone had tasted that night.

Jesus didn't want the party to break up in disgrace. He didn't want His host to be embarrassed. He didn't want the bride and groom to lose face. He was attending a joyous event, and He wanted it to stay that way. And so He shared His joy in a unique and marvelous way that people still remember today.

There was a lot of joy in Jesus' life. He shared joy with thousands. But there was also trouble and sorrow in His life—especially as He contemplated how it would end on a cruel cross.

But I want you to notice something about Jesus. Even as He faced that horrible night of sorrow, notice something. These words come right down at the end of Jesus' life, at the Last Supper:

"Then He took the cup, and gave thanks, and gave it to them, saying, 'Drink from it, all of you. For this is My blood of the new covenant, which is shed for many for the remission of sins. But I say to you, I will not drink of this fruit of the vine from now on until that day when I drink it new with you in My Father's kingdom'" (Matthew 26:27-29).

Jesus' first miracle involved giving wine to people at a wedding. At the end of His ministry, He worked another miracle to provide a Passover meal for His disciples, and during that meal, He took the cup of wine, and in drinking it, invited His disciples and you and me to come to the biggest, best celebration of them all—the wedding supper of the Lamb in heaven!

THE JOY OF JESUS

Jesus spread joy wherever He went on earth 2,000 years ago. But all the while, He was looking forward to the time—still in our future—when He would give ultimate, supreme, excitement and joy to all who would accept the wine He gives, His blood, His life, for you and me.

That makes me joyful. Whatever comes in life, nothing can take that joy away from me.

How about you? Do you have the joy of Jesus in your life? If not, won't you accept Him—and His life, His joy—today?

Joy That Reaches Me
Lonnie Melashenko

Bruce Marchiano isn't exactly a household name in our family. It doesn't even *sound* like *Melashenko*. But he has brought new joy into my life and particularly into my picture of Jesus.

As I write this chapter, it's the eve of the new millennium (2001, for the purists among us). Only a few hours ago, my wife Jeannie and I sat in church, celebrating Communion together. We are visiting family in northern California at the Paradise, California, Seventh-day Adventist church where we enjoyed a ten-year pastorate from 1981 to 1991. Because I travel so much in my ministry, I'm not often at my home church to participate in the Communion service, so we found this occasion together especially moving.

We were thrilled when we learned that the Paradise church would be celebrating Communion while we were there. There's no more profound moment in Christendom than the pure joy of taking part in the emblems representing the body and blood of our Lord

Jesus, a service He Himself instituted by command, example, and promised blessing.

I was in for a surprise. Following a brief homily by the local pastor, the congregation left the sanctuary to prepare for the Lord's Supper. Jeannie and I, together with her mother, joyfully made our way to an area set aside for families to participate in the ordinance of foot washing—the preparatory service described in the Gospel of John, chapter 13. Arm-in-arm, our threesome approached the open doorway.

That's when I noticed something that stopped me in my tracks. It was a hand-written, felt-tip-marker message scrawled on a paper grocery sack and taped to the glass door.

"When *you* take the name of Christian, friend, God puts His reputation on the line."

Wow! That is huge. Deep. Profound.

I couldn't get it off my mind for the rest of the service. And even as I sit here at my keyboard on the eve of the new millennium, it brings me to my knees and creates a lump in my throat. "Who, me?"

"Yes, you," Christ chuckles. "You, Lonnie, represent Me. Always. Everywhere."

"I wonder how many times have I turned my back on You, Lord? Denied You. Let You down. Turned and walked away. Completely *misrepresented* You at opportunities when You really counted on me to be an ambassador for heaven."

This sets me to thinking about a professional actor I met on the telephone just a few days ago. He is one of the most unforgettable characters I have ever met. Sitting in our broadcast studio I interviewed

JOY THAT REACHES ME 55

young Hollywood actor Bruce Marchiano for a Sunday *Voice of Prophecy* broadcast.

Bruce Marchiano has appeared in seven movies and numerous television shows. More recently he catapulted himself into prominence when he portrayed a Jesus of joy and laughter in the Visual Bible's movie, *Matthew*. A movie which I had only heard about, it focuses on the Gospel of Matthew and his orderly account of the good news that Jesus Christ is the Messiah.

However, in this first-of-its-kind epic, Marchiano portrays the Messiah as a smiling Jesus. Happy. Laughing. Jovial.

Frankly, because so many Hollywood movies about the Bible and Jesus leave me cold and ashamed, I don't bother to see most of them any more. But Bruce Marchiano not only plays a Jesus who has amazing love, but he also portrays a God-Man who possesses incredible joy. A Jesus who is always smiling. Laughing. The smiling Christ.

I like to be well informed during radio interviews, so I decided to read the book Bruce wrote about his experience in portraying Christ. And the night before we taped our program, I sat down to watch part of the movie. Let me tell you what happened.

Our seldom-used VCR is in our family room, so I sat down and pushed the "play" button. I was only a few minutes into the video when I called to my wife, "Wow, Jeannie! Come see this. I am so moved; I am emotionally overwhelmed."

She quietly snuggled down beside me and observed my reactions as she tenderly reached over and brushed aside a tear. Unashamedly they flowed down my cheeks. Ironically, the movie has no Hollywood drama or fiction to play on one's emotions. It has no dialogue written by producers and scriptwriters. Just straight *Scripture*, direct from the Bible. The script is direct, verbatim Gospel of Matthew discourse. But Bruce Marchiano's *delivery* of Christ's teachings profoundly, dramatically touched me. Affected me personally.

Truth is, I could hardly sleep that night. In the morning I wondered expectantly what it would be like to meet and talk to this young Hollywood actor who had so poignantly and effectively painted an entirely new picture of Christ for me. It's one thing to play the part. Quite another to walk the talk. Marchiano is a popular Christian speaker. But I pondered whether this aspiring movie star would be able to deliver the goods.

At broadcast headquarters, we dialed the number, and I met Bruce Marchiano in person on the telephone. It didn't take long to discover an authentic Christian young man whose experience of walking in the footsteps of Jesus profoundly affected and transformed his own personal life—even as a born-again Christian. Playing the part of Jesus changed his whole persona.

He took his role so seriously it became a consuming passion. He spent hours praying. Fasting. Studying his Bible. Memorizing Scripture. Thinking as Jesus must have thought as he prepared for each scene in Matthew. His playing the role of Jesus wasn't just another character role in his mind. Bruce determined to incarnate Christ. *Become* Jesus Christ.

JOY THAT REACHES ME 57

I asked him how his portrayal of the joyful Christ evolved—did this bring him a particular perspective on the joy in Jesus.

"Yeah," he said. "I don't know if it gets more special than walking in the footsteps, if you will, of the Son of the Living God—walking through the most significant events in human history. I'm an actor by profession, and I received the Lord as my Savior in 1989. In 1993, I was approached by a director who was putting the Gospel of Matthew on film. He was looking specifically for a born-again-believer-professional-actor to play Jesus, and we agreed to work together. Before I knew it, I was memorizing every word Jesus spoke as recorded by Matthew. *And looking at it all afresh.* That's a big thing right there, Lonnie."

I wondered what he meant. I liked what I was hearing from Bruce. But he excitedly pressed ahead, "You know, these Bible stories become so familiar to us. But for the first time, I had to sweep aside preconceived notions and really dig into what I would call 'The Reality of the Day,' and the reality of the Man, as opposed to the religiosity—a tall, aloof figure, you know, with arms outstretched and pristine hair and everything. And part of that whole discovery that blossomed out of that fresh look was *joy*.

"I remember my very first meeting with the director; he's an intensely praying man. And he said, 'Bruce, I have one word for you. Joy.' And he opened his Bible to Hebrews 1:9 (I'll quote it loosely): 'He was anointed with the oil of joy above His brethren.' And I remember the director said, 'Bruce, it was joy that set Him

58 THE JOY OF JESUS

apart. And I'm convinced that this is what the Lord would have us do in the film—present Jesus possibly *for the first time ever* as a *Man of joy!'* "

I observed to Bruce, "You know, as I've watched the video story of Matthew unfold, that's one of the things that jumps out and grabs you. You weren't acting. You were incarnating yourself in the person of Christ. But your smile, that magnetic warmth of joy, it just comes out and takes hold of that entire picture."

Then the surprise. Bruce replied. "You know, Lonnie, it's so interesting. I was always typecast in dark rolls—sinister looks, dark looks—before I knew the Lord."

"Is that right?" I asked incredulously.

"Yeah. So joy was never part of the program."

"But Bruce, watching your movie. . . . it's kind of like you can't wipe the smile off this Guy's face, He's always so happy!"

"Lonnie, that's the thing about joy. It's a thing you can't just wipe off your face or out of your heart. And you know, interestingly enough, when the director said that word *joy* to me, it was a bit of a surprise. I had never thought of Jesus as joyous. But I took that word he gave me and presented it to the Lord in prayer. And I took it to my reading of the Word, and suddenly I saw joy everywhere—just explosive joy. And then you think about Jesus and the Last Supper—and again I don't remember exactly the words, but He says, 'I've done these things so that My joy might be in you, so that your joy might be complete.' And we talk about the joy of our salvation. So Lonnie, *joy is definitely part of Jesus' program!"*

So the secret leaped out. Joy in Jesus. Joy in living. Bruce discovered that joy, and it became part of his life. He wasn't just acting a part, playing the role. There was more.

In Marchiano's book, *In The Footsteps of Jesus: One Man's Journey,* he talks about miraculous moments putting the movie together. Bruce's personal transformation was so electrifying it affected even non-Christian professionals during the shooting of the movie—camera men and scriptwriters and people handling lights and sound equipment. Some of the Hollywood production crew on the set at one point whispered among themselves, "Hey! Bruce isn't acting. *He is this Person, Jesus Christ!* He's projecting love and caring; he's embodying Christ right here on the set!"

Bruce confessed to me during our interview, "When I was offered the opportunity to play this part, I looked at the calendar. I had just seven weeks before the cameras were to roll. And I knew the only thing that was going to make it work was not so much for me to *pretend* to be joyous or loving or compassionate or merciful . . . but for me to *grow into* those character traits! In other words, for me—for the first time in my Christian walk—I had *to pursue Christlikeness!* Suddenly I saw the goal of my salvation here on earth; it wasn't so much that I should grow and become a good little Christian boy, but for me to grow in becoming *like Him!* And Lonnie, I can't explain to you the hours I was on my face begging the Lord to fill me with joy, to make me a joyous person. To fill me with forgiveness, mercy, compassion, and love. And hopefully that's what I brought on to the location."

To put it reverently, he pulled it off. And I say that sincerely.

Today I sit here in Paradise, California reflecting on my interview with Bruce Marchiano. Within hours, our world is about to plow straight ahead into the first year of a brand new millennium. And re-living Calvary through the Communion service—combined with my joy in Jesus re-discovered during my interview with Marchiano—causes me to realize something. It is profound, really. Bruce prepared himself for this special role and pulled it off so successfully because of one thing. He prepared for the role by immersing himself in the Word. Praying for Jesus to reveal Himself to him personally.

There's a lesson for me here. Why?

Because for Marchiano this experience resulted in such spontaneity that it has transformed not only his own life, but revolutionized future movies about Christ. It reaches out and touches me, too. It affects my life. In a new and mysterious way I find myself being drawn to that leper who came to Jesus. I can identify with him. Christ's words can transform me. Change me. Heal me. Empower me. Today. Now. If I'll just take the time to come to Jesus. Commune with Him. Pray to Him. Spend movingly memorable moments meditating and musing on my Master's marvelous ministry and mission.

In the movie, Bruce often departed from the script directives for acting moves and pre-planned gestures and allowed the spontaneity of the moment to become his guide. There were no retakes for those scenes. I'll never forget the scene where Jesus, upon healing the leper, allowed him to tackle Him with sheer ecstasy and they roll on the ground together, laughing uproariously the laughter of God—the joy of celebration—God helping people find joy in Jesus.

That's what I discovered in the movie. And that's what I discovered in meeting Bruce Marchiano in person.

It brings to focus my life. Jesus wants to do this for me. He wants to replicate this same joy in me and through me. Joy in living.

The question is this: What about my time alone spent with Jesus in Bible study and prayer? Am I immersing myself enough in the Word and praying for Jesus to reveal Himself so profoundly and personally to me that I become like Him? Am I discipling and disciplining myself to become a disciple of Christ in the truest sense of the word?

What an actor does is put himself in another person's shoes. And if he or she is good enough at it, it's worth millions—and profoundly affects millions too. Bruce determined to go a quantum step beyond acting—to guide his audience to the point of putting themselves in Jesus' shoes. Like the incident of Jesus healing the leper, a person so shockingly devastated on every level who suddenly, in the blink of an eye, saw himself liberated from that devastation. I sat there at the edge of my seat convicted: "Lord, if You could do it for him, You can do it for me too."

As we reflected on the scene of Christ healing the leper, Bruce concluded our interview with laughter. "I mean, is that a boring experience? It that a lukewarm thing? I tell you, there is nothing more exciting. And Jesus walked in that excitement every day of His life!"

My spiritual journey has been enriched by meeting a person like Bruce Marchiano. How can I put it? As one wise observer of human life once said, "Some people come into our lives, leave footprints on our hearts, and we are never *ever* the same."

Bruce, I'm thinking of that felt-tip-marker message that greeted me at Communion service yesterday. You have hung out the message on the window of your life. *God's reputation is in safe hands since you have taken the name of Christian!* It's not just a profession with you. It's character. And that's what counts.

Thank you, Bruce, for helping me re-discover Jesus. For reminding me that character counts. Thanks for bringing me joy in living!

Lasting Joy
Ken Wade

I had an interesting experience with joy while working on this series of programs. Focusing on Jesus as a Man of joy profoundly moved me, and I came to realize that I ought to have more joy in my life.

So, I decided to be joyful all the time.

Trouble was, I found it was kind of like the decision I used to make almost every day when I was a boy.

At our home in Salem, Oregon, we had a large pasture in back of our house part of which was flooded by winter rains about six months out of the year. But I loved to play out there—to chase frogs, dig holes, watch the little water bugs. Everything about the place fascinated my young mind.

I'd go out there any afternoon it wasn't raining, and every time I'd promise myself to be *very* careful this time. I'd step only on the little hummocks of grass that stuck up above the water. I wouldn't get my shoes and socks wet.

And every evening as the sun set, I'd return home with wet shoes and socks.

I soon discovered I wasn't any better at being joyful all the time than I was at keeping my socks dry.

I'd try to hit the high points, take the positive view of everything that came my way. But still things would get on my nerves, make me edgy or impatient.

I've always been moved by this sentence about Jesus, written by Ellen G. White: "The Saviour was never elated by applause, nor dejected by censure or disappointment. When He met with the greatest opposition and the most cruel treatment, He was of good courage." I've wanted to emulate that in my life.

But it doesn't always come easy.

Yet, there is an abiding joy in Jesus; just reading about Him and the way He handled life is a tremendous inspiration. It keeps me looking up. It keeps me challenged. Just that fact keeps more joy in my life because I know He wants to give me that joy—that hard-won joy that Joni talked about, that Jesus-incarnated joy that Bruce talked about.

Joy is not a natural commodity we can buy or keep in a storage bin. It's a gift; it's Jesus' gift to the world. It's a gift we must receive every day—one day at a time—from the Giver. From Jesus.

It's the joy of Jesus.

But it can be yours. And mine too.